You Woke Up Worthy

A 21-Day Self-Love Journey for Women with Big Dreams

BY BRITNY WEST

ISBN: 978-1072610236

Front cover image by Britny West

Printed by Kindle Direct Publishing
First printing edition 2019.

Contact information: info@britnywest.com

www.lifeasbritny.com

Dedication

I dedicate this book to the badass women who joined the original "I Woke Up Worthy" course back in 2017. Thank you for not only believing in me and my work, but also for your commitment to showing up for yourself on this journey. You all inspire me more than you know.

This workbook would not be here without you.

A letter from me to you:

You haven't even started this journey yet, and I'm so damn happy and proud of how far you've come. You're holding this book in your hands, because you're ready to love yourself on a deeper level than ever before and that is a very special thing!

Every single day we are bombarded with messages telling us, both directly and indirectly, that we don't measure up and that we aren't enough just the way we are.

I call bullshit!

If you're reading this I know you may not be feeling so hot about yourself right now, but I have news for you: All that is about to start changing. Pretty soon, you'll look in the mirror and see a whole new woman looking back.

Technically, she's not really new because she's been there inside you all along! I've put my heart and soul into creating this 21 day self-love experience for you, and I can't wait for you to get started already!

Enough talk from me. Just know: I am so glad you're here, and I don't take it for granted even for a second. You're why this workbook exists, beauty.

Let's get started shall we?

love, Britny

Who am I to talk about self-love?

You may be thinking to yourself, who the hell is this Britny chick and who is she to talk to me about self-love? For starters, I'm a human just like you who's also on a journey to love herself more. That's right, I won't pretend to be some guru who has it all figured out, because I'm definitely not!

What I will tell you is that over the past 6 years I've coached thousands of people on just about every topic under the sun and the root of pretty much all their problems has been a lack of real self-love. So much in your life can change just by choosing to see yourself as 100% worthy

Personally, I've battled depression and anxiety for as long as I can remember. Back in early 2013 on the heels of a massive breakup, a miscarriage, working with an abusive boss, and a slew of other crap-tastic things, I decided my life wasn't worth living anymore. I didn't feel I had a reason or a desire to live, because I didn't believe I could ever feel better about myself.

Thankfully, before I could act on those awful thoughts the voice of my higher self, whom I like to call my Inner Wise Woman, showed up to save the day.

She told me I had to find a new way to be happy. I had to learn to love myself and help others do the same. Feeling like the last person on Earth who should be helping anyone with that, I embarked on the journey anyway.

That's what led me down the path to become a self-love coach and eventually write this book. I'll be on this self-love journey for the rest of my life, but I figure why not share with you what I've learned so far?

How to use this workbook:

This workbook was once a 21-day course I hosted live with a group of incredible women I connected with online. I've adapted it here to be a 21-day guided experience to help you see yourself as 100% worthy, let go and forgive the past, set stronger boundaries, re-connect to your purpose, align your life, and pursue your big hairy audacious dreams.

Each day has a different theme partnered with prompts and exercises to help you integrate the work into your life. I also include a set of affirmations for you to say out loud in front of the mirror every day of the challenge.

Make this experience work for you and your life. If you need more time to get through everything, don't beat yourself up about it. That would be the opposite of my intention for this work! If you have to skip a day for now because life happens, please at least do the daily affirmations and 30 second self-love exercise. Those two practices alone are incredibly powerful.

At the end of this experience, my hope is that you continue to integrate these practices into your life in a way that's personalized to you and what your best life looks like.

Also - this experience is even more powerful when done with a friend or group of trusted women so feel free to include others on your journey if it feels right.

If you'd like to document your journey on social media, feel free to use the hashtag #youwokeupworthy so I can follow along too. I'd love to see your progress!

Table of Contents

Your 21 day self-love
journey starts now...

My personal commitment:

I, _____, commit to showing up with my full mind, body, and soul for this experience. By signing my name below, I am committing to completing this 21 day self- love journey. If I miss a day, I promise to not beat myself up but simply to show up the next day without shame or self-judgment.

I am worthy of this time and energy. I am worthy of a more loving relationship with myself. I know that by showing up for myself, I lead the way for other women like me to show up for themselves, too. My word is my bond.

• •
Your signature

• •
Today's date

Day 1: 100% worthy

It's unfortunate that so many of us walk around feeling like we aren't enough, just the way we are. Instead, we hustle hard to prove our worth through the things we accomplish, achieve, and do.

The truth is, every single day you wake up 100% worthy and enough. There is nothing you need to do to earn this status. In fact, there is nothing you can do to lose it.

Imagine if you woke up every day feeling like you were worthy of your desires and dreams. How would you live your life differently? What if everything you did came from a place of self-love rather than self-loathing?

You'd accomplish, achieve, and do more - but not in the name of proving yourself. You'd do it all from the perspective of wanting to expand and experience as much as you can. You'd know you are deserving of all the good things in life.

Feeling worthy is not about becoming something that you aren't already. It's about remembering who you've always been underneath your insecurities, doubts, and fears. It's about re-connecting to the truth of who you are and who you came here to be.

The intention of today's exercise is to help you get back in touch with this truth and to help you see how your life would be different if you saw yourself as 100% worthy. I have a feeling you'll be amazed at what's possible for you when you get it all down on paper!

Daily Affirmations

Repeat the following affirmations out loud 3 times while looking at yourself in the mirror:

I woke up worthy today.

Just by waking up, I'm worthy of anything my heart desires.

I am a beautiful soul, inside and out.

I love myself deeply and completely.

I am perfect at being me.

For 30 seconds, wrap your arms around your body in a hug, and feel into the emotion and experience of love. Turn up the volume of the feeling as much as you can. It may be helpful to visualize a golden or pink light pouring over you as you feel into the love.

How would your life be different if you saw yourself as 100% worthy? What would you be doing? What would you be creating? What would you be experiencing?

Find a picture of yourself from when you were a little girl and paste it here. Place descriptive words and loving phrases all around her. She is 100% worthy.

Day 2: "I'll feel worthy when..."

Do you believe there are conditions you must meet to be worthy? Do you believe you need to be, do, and have certain things in order to prove yourself? If so, you're not alone!

It's no wonder you feel this way when as a society we are constantly bombarded with advertising messages telling us to buy this special cream or weight loss drink or fancy new car in order to look or appear a certain way. Advertising brainwashes us into believing that we aren't enough just the way we are, and that we need other things outside of us to feel whole or complete.

Not only that, but we receive messages from people around us that we're either too little or too much. If we aren't working hard enough, we're called lazy. If we're working too hard, we're labeled as workaholics, etc. We're constantly placed in positions where we cannot win for losing, but only because we choose to believe that our worth is conditional on something outside of us.

The truth is you wake up worthy every single day. There is nothing you can do to change that. If you have big dreams and things you want to do in this world, please do them and enjoy the process! But don't for a second think that those things are what make you enough. You have and always will be enough as you are. Nothing to prove here!

Today's prompt will help you uncover the ways you fall prey to conditional worthiness. It will help you see where you've been trying to prove yourself so that you can let go of that need and pursue what actually lights you up.

Daily Affirmations

Repeat the following affirmations out loud 3 times while looking at yourself in the mirror:

I woke up worthy today.

Just by waking up, I'm worthy of anything my heart desires.

I am a beautiful soul, inside and out.

I love myself deeply and completely.

I am perfect at being me.

For 30 seconds, wrap your arms around your body in a hug, and feel into the emotion and experience of love. Turn up the volume of the feeling as much as you can. It may be helpful to visualize a golden or pink light pouring over you as you feel into the love.

What conditions do you place on your worthiness? Who do you feel you must be? What do you feel you must do, accomplish, or achieve in order to be enough?

Continued...

Day 3: Forgiving yourself

If you've never done any kind of forgiveness work, let me tell you today (and tomorrow) are going to be powerful days for you! Forgiveness is free, but it's often the last thing we want to do when it comes to healing.

A lot of people think forgiveness means you're saying what happened wasn't painful when it really was. In truth, forgiveness is just a way to let go of the energy surrounding certain events and experiences so you can move on with your life. It frees you from feeling the effects of something that happened in the past over and over again on repeat.

Forgiveness is for you, and believe it or not the person you must start with forgiving is yourself. The person you are hardest on is you. The person you judge and shame the most is you. The person it's often the hardest to forgive is you.

Today I'm gonna guide you through a forgiveness exercise called H'oponopono. It's a Hawaiian forgiveness ritual, and it's super simple yet totally powerful.

This process will likely feel emotional, so let the tears flow if they come. Take your time, and don't rush yourself. Tomorrow you'll be focusing on forgiving others.

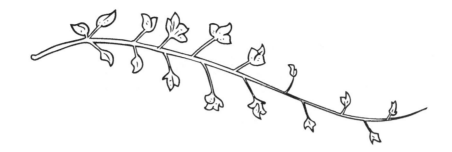

H'oponopono Hawaiian Forgiveness Ritual

Step 1

Set aside at least an hour where you won't be interrupted.

Step 2

Set the intention to forgive and heal. Are you truly ready to forgive?
You can even light a candle to honor the space.

Step 3

Write down everything you need to forgive yourself for. Go as far
back as you can remember. (journaling space on next page)

Step 4

Say the H'oponopono forgiveness prayer aloud for each item on your
list - "I'm sorry. I love you. I forgive you."

Step 5

Visualize/feel the heavy weight of the shame/guilt leaving your body
and then feel your power returning.

Daily Affirmations

Repeat the following affirmations out loud 3 times while looking at yourself in the mirror:

I woke up worthy today.

Just by waking up, I'm worthy of anything my heart desires.

I am a beautiful soul, inside and out.

I love myself deeply and completely.

I am perfect at being me.

For 30 seconds, wrap your arms around your body in a hug, and feel into the emotion and experience of love. Turn up the volume of the feeling as much as you can. It may be helpful to visualize a golden or pink light pouring over you as you feel into the love.

What do you need to forgive yourself for?

Continued...

How did it feel to forgive yourself? What came up for you? Free write whatever you'd like to help you process your experience

Day 4: Forgiving others

Just like yesterday, today's focus is all about forgiveness. Only this time you'll be forgiving others for how they've contributed to your feelings of unworthiness or not enough-ness.

If you put your heart and soul into yesterday's work, you know now how powerful forgiveness can be when you're truly ready to forgive.

Today will be just as powerful.

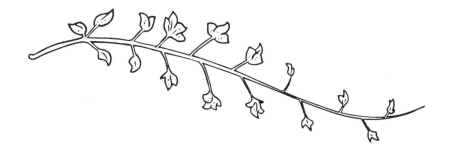

H'oponopono Hawaiian Forgiveness Ritual

Step 1

Set aside at least an hour where you won't be interrupted.

Step 2

Set the intention to forgive and heal. Are you truly ready to forgive?
You can even light a candle to honor the space.

Step 3

Write down everything you need to forgive yourself for. Go as far
back as you can remember. (journaling space on next page)

Step 4

Say the H'oponopono forgiveness prayer aloud for each item on your
list - "I'm sorry. I love you. I forgive you."

Step 5

Visualize/feel the heavy weight of the shame/guilt leaving your body
and then feel your power returning.

Daily Affirmations

Repeat the following affirmations out loud 3 times while looking at yourself in the mirror:

I woke up worthy today.

Just by waking up, I'm worthy of anything my heart desires.

I am a beautiful soul, inside and out.

I love myself deeply and completely.

I am perfect at being me.

For 30 seconds, wrap your arms around your body in a hug, and feel into the emotion and experience of love. Turn up the volume of the feeling as much as you can. It may be helpful to visualize a golden or pink light pouring over you as you feel into the love.

Who has contributed to your feelings of unworthiness? Who do you need to forgive in order to move forward?

Continued...

How did it feel to forgive everyone on your list? What came up for you? Free write whatever you'd like to help you process your experience

Day 5: Your love languages

I know the last two days' prompts have been very deep, so today we'll be doing something a bit more lighthearted and fun!

In Dr. Gary Chapman's book, The Five Love Languages, he shares that there are 5 ways we express and experience love: words of affirmation, acts of service, physical touch, quality time, and receiving gifts. While Dr. Chapman focuses mainly on romantic acts of love in his book, I figure why not apply the concept of love languages to self-love and how we express love to ourselves?

Today's prompt is to take the love languages quiz, and find out your top 3 love languages.. There are a few online quizzes that are free and easy to take. Alternatively, you can read through the descriptions on the next page and feel into which you believe are your preferred love languages.

Once you have an idea of which self-love activities fit your love language best, choose at least one thing you'll do for yourself today that will help you feel loved on and cherished.

If you're feeling resistant to this, remember you don't have to do anything to earn love. You are worthy of being treated well every single day, and who better to give you love than yourself!

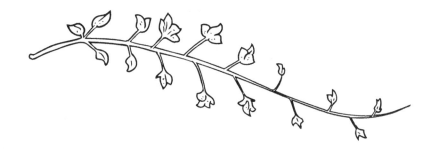

the 5 love languages (self-love edition)

Physical Touch

You're a very sensual person, preferring to feel and experience pleasure and love through your bodily senses. You love to move your body through exercise, dance, and sport. You're very affectionate with the people you love. You feel drawn to certain fabrics, because you love the way they feel on your skin. Massages, body movement, bubble baths, and self-pleasure are the ultimate self-care rituals for you.

Words of Affirmation

Words hold a lot of meaning for you, and hearing the right words can totally make your day. You're a great communicator and enjoy giving and receiving compliments and kind words. You also love being verbally acknowledged for your accomplishments. The ultimate self-care rituals for you include journaling, saying affirmations in the mirror, listing out your accomplishments/celebrations, listening to or reading inspiring messages, etc.

Acts of Service

Feeling taken care of and supported is important to you. Anything that can take a weight off your own shoulders and make your day go more smoothly is your favorite. You're a very giving person yourself, but wish more people would be as thoughtful as you are when it comes to doing favors and helping out. Recommended self-care rituals for you include delegating tasks or hiring out services (e.g. cooking, cleaning, running errands, etc.), upgrading to VIP level treatment, saying no more often, & having time to "do nothing" guilt-free.

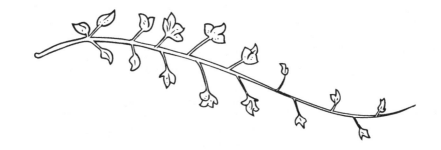

the 5 love languages (self-love edition)

Receiving Gifts

You love thoughtful touches and recieving tokens of appreciation and love. Surprises and finding unexpected "happy" gifts in the mail totally make your day (or even your week)! You're a very sentimental person and cherish what your loved ones gift you, no matter how big or small. Recommended self-care rituals for you include shopping for yourself, treating yourself to your favorite monthly box subscriptions, buying yourself flowers, and setting up an Amazon wish list of your favorite things so the people in your life know what you really want.

Quality Time

You value experiences and memories over anything else on this list. You appreciate things, but for you nothing beats being in the moment - especially with the people you care about. You're a very nostalgic person and have a habit of re-living old memories in your mind. You love taking photos and documenting the precious moments of your life. Recommended self-care rituals for you include booking a trip somewhere exciting, going out and doing something fun with someone you love spending time with, meditation, visualization, booking a class to learn or experience something new, calling someone you miss on the phone, having a "me" day where you spend your time however you want, etc.

Daily Affirmations

Repeat the following affirmations out loud 3 times while looking at yourself in the mirror:

I woke up worthy today.

Just by waking up, I'm worthy of anything my heart desires.

I am a beautiful soul, inside and out.

I love myself deeply and completely.

I am perfect at being me.

For 30 seconds, wrap your arms around your body in a hug, and feel into the emotion and experience of love. Turn up the volume of the feeling as much as you can. It may be helpful to visualize a golden or pink light pouring over you as you feel into the love.

What are your top 3 love languages? How can you show yourself love using your primary love languages?

You are perfect just
the way you are.

Day 6: Reflection

You're almost 1/3 of the way through this 21 day experience! Yass! I'm so freaking proud of you for staying committed to your self-love journey! As you've seen already this work is not always rainbows and roses, but it's totally worth it when you see how far you've come.

Today, your only prompt aside from your daily affirmations (please do those!) is to take some time to reflect on what you've uncovered and learned about yourself so far. On the next page I've created some space for you to free write your thoughts and any a ha! moments that have surfaced.

Don't skip today as it's just as (if not more) important than the more active days. It's an opportunity to integrate your experience on a deeper level. My intention for you throughout this journey is not only to love yourself more than ever before but to keep that going well past completing this 21 day workbook.

Daily Affirmations

Repeat the following affirmations out loud 3 times while looking at yourself in the mirror:

I woke up worthy today.

Just by waking up, I'm worthy of anything my heart desires.

I am a beautiful soul, inside and out.

I love myself deeply and completely.

I am perfect at being me.

For 30 seconds, wrap your arms around your body in a hug, and feel into the emotion and experience of love. Turn up the volume of the feeling as much as you can. It may be helpful to visualize a golden or pink light pouring over you as you feel into the love.

Reflection: What have you learned from this experience so far? Have you had any a-ha! moments?

Continued...

Day 7: Growing is not "fixing"

When you approach personal development and self-help from a space of "I'm not good enough" and "I need fixing," it can leave you feeling worse off than ever. Here's why: Growing is not about "fixing." You, my dear, are not broken therefore, you don't need to be "fixed."

Take a moment to let that truth sink in. Can you feel your shoulders relaxing and leaving your ears as they go back down to where they belong? The truth is, it's very possible to love yourself for who you are right now while also holding a vision of the person you'd like to become.

In my experience, personal growth is more about letting go of what's not working rather than trying to change who you are deep down. It's about letting the highest version of yourself come out to play! She is already inside you, but is likely buried under all kinds of beliefs and ideas about yourself that aren't actually true.

In today's exercise you'll be taking a bird's eye view of your life as it stands now, using the Wheel of Life tool on the next page. I encourage you to use this as a guide showing you where you want to go rather than as a problem that needs "fixing." Growing into the person you're meant to be is a journey, not a destination. The more you can love yourself as you are right now, the more easily you'll get where you want to be. Sounds weird, but it's the truth I pinky swear.

Wheel of Life

For each life area, give yourself a score from 1-10. Next, shade in the number of corresponding lines for each area (using different colors helps). Which areas did you score the highest in? The lowest? Select 1-2 areas you'd like to increase your score in and place a star by them.

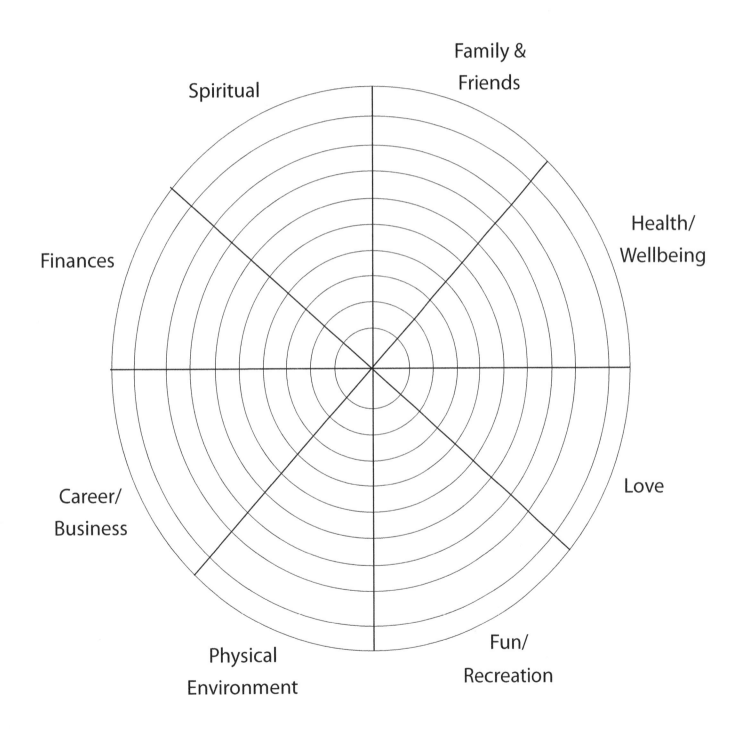

Daily Affirmations

Repeat the following affirmations out loud 3 times while looking at yourself in the mirror:

I woke up worthy today.

Just by waking up, I'm worthy of anything my heart desires.

I am a beautiful soul, inside and out.

I love myself deeply and completely.

I am perfect at being me.

For 30 seconds, wrap your arms around your body in a hug, and feel into the emotion and experience of love. Turn up the volume of the feeling as much as you can. It may be helpful to visualize a golden or pink light pouring over you as you feel into the love.

How do you feel about your Wheel of Life? Did any of your scores surprise you? Why?

Which 2-3 areas did you score the highest in? Why do you think that is? How can you continue to maintain or even raise these scores?

Where in your life could you use an upgrade? How can you work on these areas without falling into the trap of trying to "fix" yourself?

Day 8: Finding alignment

Part of your worthiness and self-love journey is letting go of the things in your life that no longer feel good. If you take a look around at your current work, relationships, home environment, health, etc. and you feel totally unfulfilled this is a sign that there is room to get into more alignment.

Alignment is a fancy way of saying that things feel right. When you're aligned, life just seems to flow organically. You feel like you're on the right path towards becoming the person you really are deep down. Notice I didn't say anything about doing what everyone else expects of you. If you feel like you're living someone else's version of happiness, fulfillment, and success then you're not living in alignment.

Before you start feeling all funky about the way things are now, I want to remind you that you hold a lot more power over these things than you realize. You may not be able to change everything that no longer feels right to you overnight, but you can certainly start making little upgrades over time. When you you look at your life and feel, "Yes! This is me!" - you know you're getting somewhere.

Today's prompt will help you take stock of what's working and what's not working so you can start taking those steps now versus later.

Daily Affirmations

Repeat the following affirmations out loud 3 times while looking at yourself in the mirror:

I woke up worthy today.

Just by waking up, I'm worthy of anything my heart desires.

I am a beautiful soul, inside and out.

I love myself deeply and completely.

I am perfect at being me.

For 30 seconds, wrap your arms around your body in a hug, and feel into the emotion and experience of love. Turn up the volume of the feeling as much as you can. It may be helpful to visualize a golden or pink light pouring over you as you feel into the love.

What feels good in your life right now? What doesn't feel so good, and if given the choice, you'd let it go? What do you feel is missing that you'd love to add more of?

What are 3 action steps you can take in the next 30 days to start working towards a more aligned life? How committed are you to making this happen?

Day 9: loving yourself anyway

When you see yourself and your life through lenses of "not enough" and scarcity, you miss out on all the good stuff. Judging others, complaining, and seeing problems all around you are all signs that you're not seeing through the eyes of love. Instead, you're seeing through the eyes of fear.

The groovy thing about feeling worthy and loving yourself more is that it not only changes how you see yourself but also how you see the world. That's because when you're judging and complaining and seeing only "the bad," what you're really doing is mirroring your inner world onto your outer world. When you feel good, you see the good. When you feel bad, you only see the bad. Makes sense, right?

I bet you didn't realize you were that powerful, huh? Well, you are!

The intention of today's prompt is to put on your rose-tinted glasses and choose to go about your day looking at the world and your experiences through the lenses of love.

When something happens that would normally make you feel unworthy, anxious, irritated, etc. say out loud or to yourself, "I choose to see love instead of this." Think of all the ways this situation can be perceived as a positive. If you're judging yourself, make sure to see yourself as lovable too.

Remember that it is a choice to see love in any moment. It's a choice to feel good or to allow yourself to stay in feeling not so good. You can't control what others do nor a lot of what's going on in the world, but you can absolutely control your reaction to it.

Practice seeing through the lenses of love, and your entire life will transform right in front of your eyes (no pun intended hehe).

Daily Affirmations

Repeat the following affirmations out loud 3 times while looking at yourself in the mirror:

I woke up worthy today.

Just by waking up, I'm worthy of anything my heart desires.

I am a beautiful soul, inside and out.

I love myself deeply and completely.

I am perfect at being me.

For 30 seconds, wrap your arms around your body in a hug, and feel into the emotion and experience of love. Turn up the volume of the feeling as much as you can. It may be helpful to visualize a golden or pink light pouring over you as you feel into the love.

Write about a time when you judged yourself harshly. Given the opportunity to go back in time, how would you have reacted differently if you were seeing yourself through the eyes of love and compassion?

Reflect on your day today. What was it like to consciously choose to see through rose-tinted glasses? What would happen if you did this every day?

You are enough.

Day 10: Standards and boundaries

Often, when you aren't feeling so good about yourself you tolerate things that feel okay in the short run but really don't represent the vision you have for yourself long term. You soften your boundaries in order to not seem selfish or bitchy. You say yes over and over again, when really you mean no.

You wear busy like a badge of honor, when inside you're exhausted and resentful that no one else is picking up the slack but you. You do what no longer feels good, because it doesn't feel safe to set new expectations and to not do what you've always done. The worst thing you can imagine is feeling like you're letting people down and disappointing those you care about.

However, the most loving thing you can do for yourself and the ones you love is to set strong boundaries and then actually honor them. You are not selfish for having needs. You're a person, too and you deserve to receive the same respect and care you give to everyone else.

At first, this will be scary as hell. People will likely push back, because they aren't accustomed to the new way. You'll find out quickly who your true friends are, and also who really isn't. If you lose friends because they choose not to respect your boundaries, they were never really friends to begin with. They were energy vampires, taking all they could get from you without having to give anything back in return.

A genuine friendship is a mutually beneficial energy exchange where both people feel loved, seen, and supported. If you're always the person giving but never receiving in all of your relationships, that's a problem. You are worthy of more than one-sided relationships!

Today's exercise is to get clear on what you'll no longer tolerate in your life and relationships so you can set new boundaries and standards that truly respect and honor the person you are becoming in this process.

Remember to tune into the fact that you are 100% worthy of your needs and desires. Boundary setting is hard in the beginning, but it does get easier the more you do it.

Daily Affirmations

Repeat the following affirmations out loud 3 times while looking at yourself in the mirror:

I woke up worthy today.

Just by waking up, I'm worthy of anything my heart desires.

I am a beautiful soul, inside and out.

I love myself deeply and completely.

I am perfect at being me.

For 30 seconds, wrap your arms around your body in a hug, and feel into the emotion and experience of love. Turn up the volume of the feeling as much as you can. It may be helpful to visualize a golden or pink light pouring over you as you feel into the love.

"I'm no longer willing to tolerate…"(Free write whatever comes up for you around this)

Continued...

"My new standards are..." (What would you like to be your new normal? What boundaries are you setting?)

Day 11: Creating space

Are you hanging onto a lot of old stuff? You'd be surprised at how heavy all that old energy can be, and how much energetic weight is released by simply decluttering your environment (both physical and digital)! When you clear out all this out, you free up space for the new to come in.

For example, if you're starting a new business but you still have all your old biz cards and ephemera lying around it's likely gonna impact your productivity in the new opportunity. If you're focused on manifesting your soul mate, but you still have boxes of your ex-partner's stuff hidden away in your closet, it sends the message that you're not actually ready to meet him or her.

Someone I knew was focused on attracting new love into her life, and it wasn't until she cleaned out her nightstands that she realized her divorce papers were in them! If that's not a repellent to new love, I'm not sure what is!

In any case, whatever your desires and dreams are for the future you'll want to make some space for them in your environment. Don't hang onto old stuff that has no place in your new life. Let it go! Let it go! It may be emotional, but it will be so worth it once you start attracting all the things you truly desire.

Today's prompt is to identify what needs to be cleared out of your space and to get started on the process. If it feels overwhelming to clear out everything at once, set a challenge to get rid of 3 things a day for 30 days or think of some other way to break it down in a way that doesn't feel quite so much of a burden.

You've got this!

Daily Affirmations

Repeat the following affirmations out loud 3 times while looking at yourself in the mirror:

I woke up worthy today.

Just by waking up, I'm worthy of anything my heart desires.

I am a beautiful soul, inside and out.

I love myself deeply and completely.

I am perfect at being me.

For 30 seconds, wrap your arms around your body in a hug, and feel into the emotion and experience of love. Turn up the volume of the feeling as much as you can. It may be helpful to visualize a golden or pink light pouring over you as you feel into the love.

What in your life could use a good cleanse? (e.g. inbox, paid subscriptions/apps, computer files, social media, closet, body/skincare products, food choices, relationships, beliefs/mindset)

Continued...

Day 12: Purpose & creativity

I sincerely believe that every single human on this Earth is here for a reason. All of our lives have meaning and purpose, which is why we all feel drawn to certain things more than others. We all have unique gifts, talents, and interests that we just can't help but pursue. When we don't pursue what sets our souls on fire, we feel our lives lack meaning. We feel like something is missing, and we feel lost.

I've definitely had times in my life where I've felt this way. When I look back, I can see clearly the seasons of my life where I was not living in alignment with my truth.Instead, I was either doing what others expected of me or what I felt was the safest option at the time. It was in those times that I felt the most lost and disconnected from myself.

It takes courage to step out of what you're familiar with and move towards what you're truly meant to be doing, but the outcome more than outweighs the fear. You are a creator, and you are meant to create. You don't have to quit your job and go live in the forest making art in an abandoned hut to pursue your purpose. Although by all means go do that if that's what feels right for you! The important thing is to make time for what you're passionate about doing.

It's okay if you aren't totally sure what your purpose is yet. Follow the breadcrumbs. The breadcrumbs being the topics and activities that you can't stop thinking about. If you feel drawn to something it's because you see yourself in it, even subconsciously.

Imagine if Freddie Mercury had never pursued his dreams to be a musician? He certainly didn't play into society's expectations of what a lead singer looked like, but he didn't let that stop him did he? He became one of the most iconic singers and songwriters in history, all because he had the courage to overcome his fears.

Now it's your turn! For today's prompt you'll be exploring your passions, interests, and inspirations so you can start following your purpose too.

Daily Affirmations

Repeat the following affirmations out loud 3 times while looking at yourself in the mirror:

I woke up worthy today.

Just by waking up, I'm worthy of anything my heart desires.

I am a beautiful soul, inside and out.

I love myself deeply and completely.

I am perfect at being me.

For 30 seconds, wrap your arms around your body in a hug, and feel into the emotion and experience of love. Turn up the volume of the feeling as much as you can. It may be helpful to visualize a golden or pink light pouring over you as you feel into the love.

What do you feel passionate about? What inspires you?
What would you create if you weren't afraid?

Continued...

Create a dream board in the space below using your
favorite images and words.

Day 13: Meet your inner wise woman

Inside, you have two voices: The abundance-minded, loving voice of your Inner Wise Woman (higher self) and the scarcity-minded, fearful voice of your Inner Mean Girl (ego mind). Your Inner Mean Girl is the part of you that feels unworthy and not enough, while your Inner Wise Woman knows she's 100% worthy and is so much more than enough.

Unfortunately, the voice that is the loudest is the one we choose to believe and listen to most often. For most of us, that's the voice of our Inner Mean Girl. She's the one who is constantly judging and criticizing you. The easiest way to identify which voice is which is to ask, "is this thought coming from a place of fear or love?" Your Inner Wise Woman will always speak from a place of love while your Inner Mean Girl will always speak from a place of fear.

Your Inner Wise Woman is the highest version of yourself. She's the voice of your intuition and the part of you that feels drawn to take the uncertain, unknown paths in life. The paths that ultimately lead you become to the person you were born to be.

Your Inner Mean Girl isn't all bad, though. She has good intentions, even if she can be hurtful in her delivery. She just wants you to avoid pain and bad things happening. You can't get rid of her, because she is also a part of you.

For that reason, it's important that you make peace with her while also no longer allowing her to run the show anymore. You can consciously choose to turn up the volume of your Inner Wise Woman's voice and receive her guidance more often. It takes intention and a bit of patience in the beginning, but it's so worth the effort!

The easiest way to meet your Inner Wise Woman is to create time for her each day. You can start by setting a timer for 10 minutes, closing your eyes, and setting the intention to listen and connect to her. Don't worry if you don't "hear" anything the first few times. Sometimes an idea will simply pop into your head or you'll just feel more supported by an unseen energy. It's all valuable. Try not to judge your experience. Just allow and receive.

After doing this, reflect and write about your experience and any messages you received from her. You can also create a collage of images and words that you feel represent your higher self so you can put a "face" to your Inner Wise Woman. I've created space in this workbook for you to do that, too.

So are you ready to meet her?

Daily Affirmations

Repeat the following affirmations out loud 3 times while looking at yourself in the mirror:

I woke up worthy today.

Just by waking up, I'm worthy of anything my heart desires.

I am a beautiful soul, inside and out.

I love myself deeply and completely.

I am perfect at being me.

For 30 seconds, wrap your arms around your body in a hug, and feel into the emotion and experience of love. Turn up the volume of the feeling as much as you can. It may be helpful to visualize a golden or pink light pouring over you as you feel into the love.

Describe your Inner Wise Woman. What is her personality/energy like? What is she wearing? Where does she spend her time? How does she spend her time? What does she have to teach you?

Continued...

Draw or create a collage of images that represent your Inner Wise Woman.

Day 14: Reflection

You're now 75% of the way through this experience. WOOOO HOOO!! You are seriously rocking it out. You may not realize what a big deal it is to have gotten this far, but I really hope you're celebrating yourself. Your commitment is not for the faint of heart, and yet here you are doing the damn thing!

I sincerely hope this experience has helped you feel better about the person you are right here in this moment. It's so important on this journey to constantly be celebrating how far you've come in this process rather than on how far you have to go.

Today, your only prompt aside from your daily affirmations (please do those!) is to take some time to reflect on what you've uncovered and learned about yourself so far. On the next page I've created some space for you to free write your thoughts and any a ha! moments that have surfaced.

Don't skip today as it's just as (if not more) important than the more active days. It's an opportunity to integrate your experience on a deeper level. My intention for you throughout this journey is not only to love yourself more than ever before but to keep that going well past completing this 21 day workbook.

Daily Affirmations

Repeat the following affirmations out loud 3 times while looking at yourself in the mirror:

I woke up worthy today.

Just by waking up, I'm worthy of anything my heart desires.

I am a beautiful soul, inside and out.

I love myself deeply and completely.

I am perfect at being me.

For 30 seconds, wrap your arms around your body in a hug, and feel into the emotion and experience of love. Turn up the volume of the feeling as much as you can. It may be helpful to visualize a golden or pink light pouring over you as you feel into the love.

Reflection: What have you learned from this experience so far? Have you had any a-ha! moments?

Continued...

Day 15: Your emotional guidance system

As women we are often put down for being "too emotional" or "too sensitive," when really our emotional natures are our superpower. Emotions are simply energy in motion. TThey are neither good nor bad, and it's healthier for us to feel them than to avoid them. They are meant to flow through us rather than getting held back and stuck inside.

Personally, I still struggle with allowing myself cry more than a couple of tears before I "dry it up already." Growing up I felt the need to be the strong one and it felt weak to let my tears flow.

It requires courage and vulnerability to fully let go and express what's pent up inside, and yet it's one of the most healing things you can do. Your emotions are not an enemy to hide from. They are signposts showing you where you wanna go and how you want to feel next. When you see your feelings from this perspective, it's actually quite empowering.

I think many of us are afraid to express our emotions out of fear that if we allow ourselves to feel them then they will stick around for good. It's not true, in fact, it's the opposite.

When you allow your emotions to be what they are, energy in motion, you get to choose your next emotion. You get to feel the pain or the hurt or all the good stuff too and then decide what you'd like to feel next. If a situation doesn't feel good, you now are more equipped to get out of it than you were before when you were holding everything inside. Unexpressed emotion take up a lot of space and creates stress in your body unnecessarily. It's much easier to let it flow through you as it's meant to.

Today's exercise is to tune into your body and pay attention to how you feel in this moment. Do you feel stress, anxiety, contentment, excitement, fear, sadness? Whatever it is, rather than judging it as good or bad, let yourself feel it. Turn up the volume of your emotion and fully express it. If you're angry you can even scream into a pillow if it helps you let that shit go. Give yourself space to cry, laugh, scream, or simply smile out of happiness if that is what you're feeling.

Then decide how you'd like to feel next. It's best not to go from one extreme to another as it won't feel real to you. Instead ask yourself, "what is the next step up from here? How can I feel even a little bit better than I am now? What can I do to create more of that feeling?"

Sometimes a nice dance break can really do the trick when moving towards a higher frequency emotion, but you can do whatever feels right in the moment. Reflect on your experiences on the next couple of journaling pages.

Make a commitment to yourself that you'll allow yourself to follow your body's natural emotional guidance system from this point forward.

Daily Affirmations

Repeat the following affirmations out loud 3 times while looking at yourself in the mirror:

I woke up worthy today.

Just by waking up, I'm worthy of anything my heart desires.

I am a beautiful soul, inside and out.

I love myself deeply and completely.

I am perfect at being me.

For 30 seconds, wrap your arms around your body in a hug, and feel into the emotion and experience of love. Turn up the volume of the feeling as much as you can. It may be helpful to visualize a golden or pink light pouring over you as you feel into the love.

Close your eyes and pay attention to how you feel in this moment. Are you sad, tired, nervous, happy, etc.? Allow yourself to turn the volume up on that emotion and feel it – even if it's uncomfortable. Reflect on your experience.

What was it like allowing yourself to really feel your emotion(s)?

You have nothing to prove.

Day 16: Becoming the leading lady

You know what happens when you put everyone else's needs and wants ahead of your own? You become the supporting actress rather than the leading lady of your own life. Here's the deal: Your happiness, thoughts, opinions, ideas, and insights are just as important as anyone else's. It does not make you selfish to put yourself first for once!

Hear me out: When you take everyone else off of the pedestal and instead rise up to meet them on the same level, you have so much more to offer the world. You are at your best when your needs are getting met and you're feeling happy and fulfilled. It is not your responsibility to make other people happy or to make their dreams come true.

Repeat after me, "it's not my responsibility to make anyone else happy but myself." Again, this may feel super selfish but it's totally not. It's actually more selfish to expect other people to make you happy, not to mention it's a lot of weight to carry! If more incredible people like you started putting themselves first, the world would become a much better place.

You'd show up as whole, just the way you are, rather than expecting others to complete you. Wouldn't that be an amazing feeling? Knowing that any relationship you have simply expands the happiness you already have inside?

Today's prompt is a bit of a doozy if you tend to lean on other people a lot, but I know it's going to be powerful for you.

For the next 24 hours I want you to go on an Opinion Diet where you turn inward for answers rather than asking for anyone else's opinion of feedback. Obviously if you work as part of a team, those interactions don't count. The intention of this exercise is to help you increase trust in yourself. I want you to recognize that you already know the answers deep inside if you simply allow yourself to hear them. I also want you to practice putting your needs first.

If you aren't responsible for anyone else's happiness that means no one else is responsible for yours, either. It's time to put yourself back in the leading lady role. You are responsible for your own happiness, and that is a very good thing!

Daily Affirmations

Repeat the following affirmations out loud 3 times while looking at yourself in the mirror:

I woke up worthy today.

Just by waking up, I'm worthy of anything my heart desires.

I am a beautiful soul, inside and out.

I love myself deeply and completely.

I am perfect at being me.

For 30 seconds, wrap your arms around your body in a hug, and feel into the emotion and experience of love. Turn up the volume of the feeling as much as you can. It may be helpful to visualize a golden or pink light pouring over you as you feel into the love.

Go on an Opinion Diet for at least 24 hours where instead of getting feedback or advice from others you turn inward and trust that you have the answers. Reflect here on your experience and what it taught you.

Day 17: Intention is everything

Are you a to-do list queen? If you are and it works for you, great! However, in my experience and in the work I've done with my clients I've found the "to-do list" mentality is more stressful than it is helpful.

To-do lists are often ongoing and hence, never-ending reminders of what we haven't yet done. If you're already struggling with feeling worthy and enough, the last thing you need is a sheet of paper telling you where you've come up short.

What would happen if you threw out the to-do list entirely? I know we live in the real world with real responsibilities, so don't worry I'm not suggesting you drop everything. What I am suggesting is a new approach to getting things done that has you celebrating your progress at the end of each day and feeling like you are moving forward with your dreams.

This new approach is simple yet profound, and it still only requires a piece of paper and a pen. Instead of writing a long ass to-do list of things that no human can accomplish in one single day, I suggest instead that you set 3 daily intentions.

Intention is everything. Intention puts you back in the driver's seat, because you're choosing where you'd like to focus your energy and time for the day. You may have more than 3 things you need to get done, but choose three of the most important ones so they take priority over everything else.As long as you follow through on these 3 things, you can end your day feeling like a badass instead of a failure.

Ironically, setting only 3 intentions helps you get a lot more done in a lot less time. This leaves you room to choose how you'd like to spend the rest of your day. Doesn't that feel a whole lot better than expecting yourself to do everything at once?

Today's prompt is to take a few minutes before you start your day and write down your top 3 goals for the month. Then, you'll set your 3 intentions. It's best if at least one of your intentions lines up with your goals, so you can make headway each day towards your dreams. If you do this consistently, you'll begin to look forward to this every day. It's a great way to start your day feeling excited and focused.

Are you ready? Let's do this!

Set 3 intentions for what you'd like to do/accomplish/experience today (or tomorrow if you're doing this in the evening).

You are here for a reason.

Day 18: Creating a daily practice

Today builds upon yesterday's prompt of setting 3 intentions in the morning. Today, you'll be creating your own personalized daily practice! I'm excited, because I know this will be such a game changer for you!

Creating a daily practice really sets the tone for the day ahead. It helps you stay grounded and focused on what's most important to you. Not to mention when you're intentional about how you live your life, it's a helluva lot easier to create the life you want.

What works for you may not work for someone else and vice versa so I'm not going to prescribe you a daily practice. Instead, I want you to brainstorm some activities that you can do each day that align with both your schedule and personal interests. I find it works best to have a menu of options you can pull from so you can follow through whether you have only 5 minutes or a full hour to devote to your practice.

Before you get started, I want you to make a promise to yourself that you'll show up for yourself every day with a ritual or daily practice no matter how much time you have. Even 30 seconds of sending yourself love counts on those crazy busy days. As long as you're filling your own cup each day, it all adds up!

Daily Affirmations

Repeat the following affirmations out loud 3 times while looking at yourself in the mirror:

I woke up worthy today.

Just by waking up, I'm worthy of anything my heart desires.

I am a beautiful soul, inside and out.

I love myself deeply and completely.

I am perfect at being me.

For 30 seconds, wrap your arms around your body in a hug, and feel into the emotion and experience of love. Turn up the volume of the feeling as much as you can. It may be helpful to visualize a golden or pink light pouring over you as you feel into the love.

List 10 simple activities you can do no matter where you are or how much time you have. (e.g. journaling, listening to music, diffusing essential oils, dancing, yoga, singing, going for a walk, reading a book, gratitude, etc.)

What will your daily practice look like on an ideal day? What will you do on days you have only 5 or 10 minutes to spare?

Day 19: Following through on your dreams & desires

Sometimes self-love is about being completely honest with yourself about your patterns. Like I've said before, it's definitely not all rainbows and roses. Sometimes to get what you've always wanted, you have to stop doing what you've always done. Or in this case - start doing what you haven't been doing.

It can be hard to admit when your lack of follow-through is the reason for your lack of progress, but remember, there is nothing that can take away from your worthiness. You can make mistakes and take responsibility for things you haven't been doing and be 100% worthy all at the same time.

When you aren't pursuing your passions and big hairy audacious goals it can leave you feeling like something is missing in your life. That's why today's topic is all about helping you leave that lack of follow-through far behind you.

The truth is what you've done in the past has no bearing on what you can do today or tomorrow. Even if up until now you've bounced from idea to idea getting nowhere fast, you can change that story. That's how powerful you are!

When you become the woman who follows through with what she says she's going to do, incredible things happen. You trust and believe in yourself more than ever before, your confidence grows, and there is not one thing that can stand in the way of you living your best life!

Today I want you to get clear on how you can start working towards one massive goal that means the world to you. Remember that Rome wasn't built in a day, so this won't happen overnight. Simply take some time to map out what you can do today rather than putting it off until someday. Hint: Someday doesn't exist!

Here's to having it all (fulfillment and worthiness), you incredible woman!

Daily Affirmations

Repeat the following affirmations out loud 3 times while looking at yourself in the mirror:

I woke up worthy today.

Just by waking up, I'm worthy of anything my heart desires.

I am a beautiful soul, inside and out.

I love myself deeply and completely.

I am perfect at being me.

For 30 seconds, wrap your arms around your body in a hug, and feel into the emotion and experience of love. Turn up the volume of the feeling as much as you can. It may be helpful to visualize a golden or pink light pouring over you as you feel into the love.

Reflect on what you'd be doing differently if you were the woman who followed through 100% of the time. How would your life look different than it does now?

Choose one dream, goal, or desire that's really important to you right now. Outline below how you can work towards making it a reality.

Continued...

Day 20: You're already doing it

Self-love is a journey, not a destination. I know that sounds like some cheesy quote you'd see on social media, but hear me out. The ultimate trap you could possibly fall into during this process is focusing on how far you have to go rather than how far you've already come. Remember, the whole spirit of this work is recognizing that you are already 100% worthy today. Just the way you are. Nothing you can do about it!

Even if you feel like there is a whole new level you can open up to in this work, don't forget to honor where you are right now. The more you embrace that you will never get to that elusive "there," the more loving you'll feel towards yourself. It's totally possible to love the person you are today, while also working towards creating an even better life and relationship with yourself.

Today's prompt is about looking back at who you were 5 years, 3 years, or even 1 year ago and reflecting on how far you've already come. I want you to acknowledge all of the challenges and setbacks you've triumphed against despite all odds. I want you to see just how powerful you are so that when fear rises up to greet you again, you have proof you can handle whatever it is that lies between you and your dreams.

The truth is, you're already doing it. "It" being living your best life and pursuing your purpose. Even if things look a bit messy and hairy, you're still doing the damn thing.

Never forget it!

Daily Affirmations

Repeat the following affirmations out loud 3 times while looking at yourself in the mirror:

I woke up worthy today.

Just by waking up, I'm worthy of anything my heart desires.

I am a beautiful soul, inside and out.

I love myself deeply and completely.

I am perfect at being me.

For 30 seconds, wrap your arms around your body in a hug, and feel into the emotion and experience of love. Turn up the volume of the feeling as much as you can. It may be helpful to visualize a golden or pink light pouring over you as you feel into the love.

Write an encouraging letter to yourself either 1, 3, or 5 years ago sharing with your younger self what you've learned and accomplished since that time.

You light up the world
just by being you.

Day 21: Celebrate!

You've probably picked up on the fact that I'm all about you loving who you are today rather than waiting until you feel you've "earned it," whatever that means! On this last day, I think it's fitting that we focus on celebrating YOU.

I know you're likely thinking about how to making your big goals and dreams happen already, and that's great! But don't forget that you still have a lot to celebrate now. I've said this what feels like a million times now but it bears repeating: You are 100% worthy and incredible and beautiful and amazing right here, right now.

Today, I want you to come up with a massive list of things you're celebrating about yourself and how far you've come. The goal is to list at least 21 things, but honestly I'd love it if you went even further and keep going until your hand is about to fall off from so much writing. There really is so much to celebrate about you.

Just the fact that you are here is pretty damn awesome. :)

After you make this gigantic list of celebrations, I invite you to dig deeper into why these things are worth celebrating for you. I've given you a 3 question process to help you out with this. Surface level celebration is all about what happened outside of you, but deep celebration is all about what happened inside of you. That's where the real gold lies, am I right?

Daily Affirmations

Repeat the following affirmations out loud 3 times while looking at yourself in the mirror:

I woke up worthy today.

Just by waking up, I'm worthy of anything my heart desires.

I am a beautiful soul, inside and out.

I love myself deeply and completely.

I am perfect at being me.

For 30 seconds, wrap your arms around your body in a hug, and feel into the emotion and experience of love. Turn up the volume of the feeling as much as you can. It may be helpful to visualize a golden or pink light pouring over you as you feel into the love.

Make a list of 21+ things you are celebrating about
yourself and how far you've come.

Using the following questions, dig deeper into your top 3 celebrations. "What am I celebrating?" "Why is this worth celebrating?" "Who am I becoming in this process?"

Woo hoo!! You've completed this 21 day self-love journey!
What have you learned about yourself? What have been your
major a-ha! moments? How has this experience transformed
the way you see yourself?

Continued...

You did it!

You followed through on your commitment
to loving yourself more than ever before,
and I'm so damn proud of you!

I hope you're proud, too, and I hope you'll
keep this party going a long, long time.

Because you are 100% worthy of that!

xo Britny

Made in the USA
Columbia, SC
11 September 2020